ON BALANCE

JOHN HARVEY, while perhaps best known as a writer of crime fiction – in 2007 he was awarded the CWA Cartier Diamond Dagger for sustained excellence in crime writing – has always maintained a strong involvement with poetry. In addition to 30 issues of *Slow Dancer* magazine, between 1977 and 1999 his Slow Dancer Press published 13 books of poetry and 45 pamphlets, including work by Simon Armitage, Matthew Caley, Lucille Clifton, Rebecca Goss, Lee Harwood, Libby Houston, Norbert Hirschhorn, Sharon Olds, James Schuyler and Ruth Valentine. Two collections of his own poetry, *Ghosts of a Chance* (1992) and *Bluer Than This* (1998) were followed by a new and selected poems, *Out of Silence* (2014), all published by Smith/Doorstop. His most recent collection, *Aslant*, which also features photographs by his daughter Molly Ernesting Boiling, was published by Shoestring Press in 2019.

A recipient of Honorary Doctorates from the Universities of Nottingham and Hertfordshire, in 2020 he was made an Honorary Fellow of Goldsmiths' College, University of London.

ON BALANCE

JOHN HARVEY

Shoestring Press

All rights reserved. No part of this work covered by the copyright herein may be reproduced or used in any means – graphic, electronic, or mechanical, including copying, recording, taping, or information storage and retrieval systems – without written permission of the publisher.

Printed by imprintdigital
Upton Pyne, Exeter
www.digital.imprint.co.uk

Typesetting and cover design by The Book Typesetters
hello@thebooktypesetters.com
07422 598 168
www.thebooktypesetters.com

Published by Shoestring Press
19 Devonshire Avenue, Beeston, Nottingham, NG9 1BS
(0115) 925 1827
www.shoestringpress.co.uk

First published 2023
© Copyright: John Harvey
© Cover artwork: Molly Ernestine Boiling

The moral right of the author has been asserted.

ISBN 978-1-915553-28-7

ACKNOWLEDGEMENTS

Thanks are due to the editors of the following - *Acumen*, *London Grip*, *The North* - in which some of these poems first appeared. My thanks also to fellow poets - Alan Brooks, Norbert Hirschhorn, Peter Sansom, Craig Smith and Ruth Valentine - for advice and inspiration, and, of course, to my publisher, John Lucas. Scarce a day goes by when I don't take a volume of Robert Hass' poetry down from the shelf; likewise Lee Harwood, Frank O'Hara, James Schuyler – my masters.

CONTENTS

Setting Sail	1
Doc Watson	2
Early Autumn	3
First Love	4
College Days	5
Funeral	7
Bebop Nights	8
Time (& Time Again)	9
Cornwall	10
Rananim	11
On Balance	12
South of Sacramento	14
On Reading Peter Sansom's 'Lanyard'	15
On Reading Peter Sansom's 'Lanyard' II	16
Rome, 1962	17
Paris Again	18
Blessed	19
Kestrel	20
Crow	21
Losing You	22
Last Poem	24

SETTING SAIL

Wind troubles the water,
tangles and untangles the reeds;
a lone swan slides past, unperturbed.

I came here with my father
to sail the yacht he'd crafted
lovingly all summer;
a gift on my winter birthday.

The wind carried it proudly
to the centre and left it there,
marooned.

I used to see him, my father,
each time I looked in the mirror -
loving, reproachful, regret in his eyes.

Now all I see is my own face
staring back at me;
uncertain, anxious -
waiting for the right wind.

DOC WATSON

Blind since the age of two
Doc Watson fingerpicks his way
through 'Bonaparte's Retreat'
at impossible speed

Outside
swallows swoop and swerve
between rooftops,
some inner vision
guiding them back through
thousands of miles to home.

EARLY AUTUMN

The first leaves curl inward
tinged with brown;
first conkers on the ground.

A pyramid of ravens
rises on the wind.

Getz's saxophone winds its way
sinuous and not a little cold
around the sinews of the tune

We stamp our feet
reach for that extra layer,
look upward in search of the sun.

FIRST LOVE
for Dorothy

So this is how first love finally ends:
a phone call
one otherwise unremarkable
February afternoon

"She'd have wanted you to know…"

My path across the Heath
this morning
haphazard and slow

Sixty years or so
since first I felt your breath
fall warm upon my face
folded your body into mine.

COLLEGE DAYS

The street in New Cross
where I went to college
is littered with time wasted
time lost

Windows boarded up
posters torn down
my hand reaching back
in vain across the years

It was all so long ago, another age;
when visiting your ladies' place of residence,
a guest at your hall formal,
meant wearing suit and tie,
accepting warm sherry from a tray,
before moving inexpertly round the floor,
longing for the waltz when I could hold you close;
and later, in the guise of a chaste good night,
pressed up against the roughcast of some darkened wall,
kiss until our mouths were numb.

All that first year we sat across
from one another in lectures, spent
evenings in the library, studying;
lived in each other's thoughts,
each other's gaze; when time and space
allowed, in each other's arms.
Time spent imagining life together,
everything down to which books we'd read,
which newspapers, which magazines,
how many children, what make of car.

We thought of it as love and most probably it was:
it had, after all, along with the all-too obvious pleasure
a few requisite moments of pain.

"I love you" …
it seemed so easy to say and to believe;
then, at the end of that year,
without a word, it was over.

Good friends saved you - that
and your Northern stalwartness
your natural strength and pride.
You found someone else to like,
to love, or likely he found you.
Cherished you for what you are,
loved you, I trust, as you deserved.

We chose the paths we took
and in the end the paths took us.

FUNERAL

Clouds this morning
like a Constable painting;
brush strokes loose & limber
promising rain.

Seeking safety, a moorhen
darts across the pond and
disappears into the reeds.

At your funeral,
the service streamed
due to the pandemic,
I see for the first time
your children, now fully grown.

A jagged triangle of blue
breaks through the clouds,
its reflection in the water
faint but clear. You ease
in and out of memory unbidden,
impossible to hold or touch.

BEBOP NIGHTS
for Jim Burns & David Kresh

On bebop nights flattened fifths
flare up like firecrackers over Little Italy,
while on the edge of Chinatown
the line outside the Flamingo
edges anxiously closer
as below the Blue Flames
sound-check their way
through 'Moody's Mood for Love',
the throb of Hammond organ
rising through basement walls
and out onto the expectant street.

'In Bebop Nights', David Kresh, from *Turn Off or Use Opener*, Blue House Press, 2007

TIME (& TIME AGAIN)

Now it's Georgie, relaxed, singing
'Funny How Time Slips Away',
the needle catching in the groove
whenever the vocal breaks
and hands over to the horns

What was once a basement
busy with the shuffle of bodies
is now a blue plaque on an outside wall

Across the room, your wine glass
has left a pattern of fading rings

I conjure up a few faint bars
of saxophone, searching for
some kind of coda

Outside, the night is drawing close,
the outline of your footsteps
frozen in the snow.

CORNWALL
Night

Driving back across the moor
a barn owl
is caught for an instant
in the headlights

A shelf of cloud
black as anthracite
over the sea

The only sounds
the grumbling of my old heart;
your breathing
close in the cloistered dark.

RANANIM

The garden gives way onto fields,
the fields, five of them, onto the sea:
the sky this morning a mottled grey,
the sea itself, indifferent,
flat as the eye can see.

When Lawrence lived here
he envisaged a community of writers,
a republic of letters bound by friendship.

In the meantime he made furniture,
planted a garden, grappled with
the final pages of '*Women in Love*';
dashed Frieda's head against the wall
instead of his own.

We pull on our waterproofs
and walk up the lane;
flag down the bus into town,
wary of no more than rain.

Just sometimes, while you are sleeping,
I venture quietly downstairs,
run my fingers along a painted chest of drawers,
the back of a chair;
breathe in the shallow air.

ON BALANCE

Good, she says, good, good,
scrolling down her screen -
the second Wednesday of the month,
my regular session with Dr McGregor,
consultant, medical oncology -
Kidneys, liver, all clear, PSA fine.
And you're feeling okay? No pain?
A shake of the head. No pain.
Well then, angling her chair,
it seems to me, for the present
we have your disease under control.
And longer term? I read the hesitation in her eyes.
On balance? She smiles.
Let's just say I'll see you again in four weeks' time.
And keep up with the exercise, mind.
The walking …

Out on the Heath next morning,
not too early, temperature rising;
as I climb the small incline between two ponds
I see a man I half-recognise
moving awkwardly toward me,
head shiny with sweat,
a generous tilt to his walk,
and instead of, as would be usual,
nodding and passing by, we decide
to stop, catch a breath, lean on our sticks.
I glance in the direction of his leg.
Polio, when I was eleven or twelve,
been a bastard ever since.
He raises his stick, be lost without this;
take a tumble down there, like as not, not get up.

Balance at our age is everything:
like a perfect sentence depending
on that all-important comma,
that semi-colon; everything up to
and including the final full stop

SOUTH OF SACRAMENTO
for Cathy

We are on a bus
somewhere south of Sacramento
and you are crying;
tears soundlessly falling,
their reflection like rain
against the window

It's night: the lights
of approaching vehicles
startle and blur

Further back in the bus
someone is quietly snoring

A small child whimpers
and is still

Your face when you turn
toward me is beautiful;
just that little puffiness around the eyes
that comes from crying.

And only gradually do I realise
these are tears of leaving:
today, tomorrow,
your rucksack strapped
firmly on your back,
tickets held fast in your hand,
the future bright in your eyes.

ON READING PETER SANSOM'S 'LANYARD'

This isn't a poem, not even close:
we were having lunch out in the garden,
and between commenting on the sunlight
reflecting back from the leaves of the ivy
and how well, newly purchased and potted,
the cosmos had taken, I leafed through Peter's book,
searching for something I might read aloud, perhaps,
though not loud enough to startle the neighbours,
and the more I read the more it seemed
like one long poem about growing up
in the middle of nowhere, or Derbyshire
as it's sometimes called; half-forgotten rooms
that people walked into and failed to walk out of,
waiting, like memories, to be discovered,
commemorated. Not a poem this, not even close.

'Lanyard', Peter Sansom, from *Lanyard*, Carcanet, 2022

ON READING PETER SANSOM'S 'LANYARD' II

Sunlight slanting through trees
I sit leafing through Peter's book again,
in awe at the ease with which
past and present elide,
time coalesces and expands,
memories filter, like chalk dust,
between the fingers of one hand.

Cold-eyed, a cormorant breaks the surface
of the water, neck wound steeply back
to swallow its catch.

Across the North Sea our daughter
is making art from blocks of ice;
the slow beauty of decline and decay:
for an instant I see my reflection in her eyes.

Abruptly the wind changes direction,
a cloud shunts its way across the sun;
I count on the fingers of one hand
the number of times I might see her again.

Peter says it better than ever I could:
Sand in our shoes and our shoes in our hands
we walk fully clothed into the sea.

I slide his book back into my pocket,
turn and begin my unsteady walk
toward home; somewhere, melting ice
drips down into a waiting cup;
water evaporates leaving salt,
the smell, faint, of fresh sea water,
the gradual turning of the tide.

ROME, 1962

Midnight. A studio
somewhere on the Via Tiburtina;
teased by a memory, Chet Baker,
trumpet hushed, quietly addresses
'These Foolish Things'

Snow clings like alabaster
to the rooftops;
a single light shines muted
along the darkened street

Behind a threadbare curtain
she is making love to an angel,
feathers scattered like half-notes
over the bare floor

In the morning all she will remember:
a snatch of melody,
small cries and a fluttering of wings.

PARIS AGAIN

Parisian morning
the radio quietly playing

We walk out for croissants
and carry them back

In their apartment
our friends are making coffee
fresh fruit on the table waiting

Beneath the rise and fall of voices
the first notes of 'Central Park Blues'
come slowly gliding

Isn't Nina Simone
wonderful?

BLESSED

The signs for Iceland and the Coop
shine bright along the high street
reflecting on pavements still slick with rain

A police car slaloms its way between
ongoing traffic, blue lights flashing

Up here, the first floor of The Parakeet
has transformed into a New York loft:
Rachael Cohen's saxophone riding,
now lyrical, now challenging,
over guitar, bass and drums

We edge forward in our seats
understanding that for these few hours
we are listening to something memorable,
truly blessed.

KESTREL

Over our heads
a kestrel scythes
the blue black sky
in search of prey

Beneath our feet
a tangle of root
and stubborn circumstance

Some count their lives
in hours, in days,
in measured silences

Eyes skyward
you squeeze my hand.

CROW

A crow, breaking cover through the trees
dislodges memories of leaving

We will remember the moment
differently

Each to our own advantage

What were tears then are tears now

The ground underfoot
                      unsure
                      uncertain

LOSING YOU

Some days I think about losing you -
think as in a dream -
not that familiar dream
of lost luggage and mislaid passports,
misread timetables and missing trains -
the delayed 14.20 from Frankfurt
to Brussels Midi that simply disappeared -
those dreams that wake us shaking
and drenched in sweat. No.
This is a dream that doesn't seem
like a dream at all.

I wake calmly from an even sleep
and when I reach my hand
to where you have been sleeping
and feel the empty space, still slightly warm,
I know, so as not to dusturb me,
you have slipped on your dressing gown
and gone quietly downstairs,
which is where I'll find you –
at the breakfast table,
freshly brewed coffee close at hand,
while you read, undisturbed.

But the cup is cold and empty save
for last night's dregs; the book
open at the same turned-down page;
back in the bedroom, your side
of the wardrobe is bare, save
for that blue and white dress
with the gathered waist
that you hated and never wore,
a buckled shoe you lost and never found.

Panicking, I run out into the street
and call and call your name;
call until one of the neighbours,
not for the first time, leads me gently
back towards the open door
and tries, in simple language, to explain.

LAST POEM
for Sarah

We climb the hill together,
my step slow, unsteady,
buttercups bright amongst
the purple haze of grass

When we reach the meadow's edge
and I stop to catch my breath,
you forge ahead, following
the slow tilt of land until,
at the opening between two lines of trees,
you stop, turn back, hold out your hand.

Close on thirty years ago,
a promise made, unspoken;
each year since then renewed.